foreword

Crisp and sweet, blueberries are a bundle of nutrition in a tasty little package. They are as good for you as they are delicious. Loaded with antioxidants, vitamins and fibre, blueberries can lower blood pressure, fight heart disease and cancer and may help improve memory.

A few blueberries in the mix can really liven up a dish. Sure, they taste great in muffins, pancakes and pie, but there is so much more you can do with this amazing little fruit. This book is here to help you expand your blueberry horizons. Try the innovative Blueberry Turkey Meatballs or Lamb Chops with Blueberry Sauce and finish the meal with a bowl of homemade Blueberry Ice Cream. Delish!

Brie and Pecan in Phyllo with Blueberry Relish

The blueberry relish really complements the toasted pecans and creamy brie nestled in a crispy pastry. Outstanding!

Frozen phyllo pastry sheets (12 inch, 30 cm, size), thawed according to package directions	3	3
Butter, melted	1/2 cup	125 mL
Pecans, toasted and chopped (see Tip, p. 64)	1/2 cup	125 mL
Brie cheese round (4 oz., 125 g), cut into 4 wedges	1	1
Cooking oil	1 tsp.	5 mL
Shallots, finely chopped	2	2
Fresh (or frozen, thawed) blueberries	2 cups	500 ml
Red (or alcohol-free) wine	1/3 cup	75 mL
Corn syrup	1/3 cup	75 mL
Red wine vinegar	1/4 cup	60 mL
Salt	1 tsp.	5 mL
White pepper, to taste		

Cut each phyllo sheet into 4 squares. Brush 3 squares with melted butter and stack them.

Sprinkle centre of stack with 1/4 of pecans. Place 1 cheese wedge on top. Gather up corners of phyllo and pinch into a pouch. Repeat steps with remaining phyllo, pecans and cheese. Bake in 350°F (175°C) oven for about 20 minutes until phyllo is lightly browned and crispy.

For the relish, heat cooking oil in a frying pan on medium. Cook shallots for 4 minutes until lightly browned.

Add blueberries and reduce heat to medium-low. Add red wine and corn syrup. Simmer for 40 minutes, stirring occasionally, until reduced to consistency of jam.

Stir in red wine vinegar. Add salt and pepper. Serve warm with phyllo pouches. Makes 4 servings.

1 serving: 572 Calories; 46 g Total Fat (16.3 g Mono, 4.6 g Poly, 22.1 g Sat); 115 mg Cholesterol; 24 g Carbohydrate (2 g Fibre, 22 g Sugar); 9 g Protein; 1074 mg Sodium

Blueberry Fruit Dip

A tangy blueberry dip that's super simple to whip up—a not-too-sweet option that both kids and adults will enjoy. Serve with fresh sliced apple, banana, mango, melon, pineapple and strawberries for dipping. This can be made a few hours before serving.

Block of cream cheese (8 oz., 250 g), softened	1	1
Fresh (or frozen, thawed) blueberries	1 cup	250 mL
Plain yogurt	1/2 cup	125 mL
Brown sugar, packed	1/4 cup	60 mL
Flaked coconut	1/4 cup	60 mL

Process all 5 ingredients in a food processor until smooth. Makes about 2 1/3 cups (575 mL).

1/4 cup (60 mL): 140 Calories; 10 g Total Fat (0 g Mono, 0 g Poly, 6 g Sat); 30 mg Cholesterol; 11 g Carbohydrate (0.5 g Fibre, 10 g Sugar); 3 g Protein; 95 mg Sodium

Spinach and Berry Salad with Honey Mustard Vinaigrette

Fresh, sweet berries add colour and just the right amount of sweetness to this elegant salad.

Unseasoned rice vinegar	1 1/2 tsp.	7 mL
Raw honey	1 tbsp.	15 mL
Dijon mustard	1 tsp.	5 mL
Salt, to taste		
Pepper, to taste		
Baby spinach leaves	3 cups	750 mL
Head of radicchio, torn into bite-size pieces	1/2	1/2
Blueberries	1/2 cup	125 mL
Sliced strawberries	1/2 cup	125 mL
Small red onion, thinly sliced	1/2	1/2
Sunflower seeds	2 tbsp.	30 mL

Combine vinegar, honey and mustard in a small bowl. Whisk well. Add salt and pepper.

Combine spinach, radicchio, blueberries, strawberries and onion in a large bowl. Drizzle with dressing and toss to coat. Sprinkle sunflower seeds over top and serve immediately. Makes 4 servings.

1 serving: 70 Calories; 1 g Total Fat (0 g Mono, 0.5 g Poly, 0 g Sat); 0 mg Cholesterol; 14 g Carbohydrate (2 g Fibre, 9 g Sugar); 2 g Protein; 40 mg Sodium

Blueberry Quinoa Salad

This tasty and colourful mix of quinoa and pine nuts is tossed with a fragrant garlic and herb dressing. The unique addition of dried blueberries stands out in fruity bites.

Water	1 1/2 cups	375 mL
Salt	1/8 tsp.	0.5 mL
Quinoa	2/3 cup	150 mL
Chopped arugula, lightly packed	2 cups	500 mL
Canned lentils, rinsed and drained	1 cup	250 mL
Diced red pepper	1/2 cup	125 mL
Dried blueberries	1/2 cup	125 mL
Grated Swiss cheese	1/4 cup	60 mL
Pine nuts, toasted (see Tip, p. 64)	1/4 cup	60 mL
Thinly sliced green onion	2 tbsp.	30 mL
Olive (or cooking) oil	3 tbsp.	45 mL
Raspberry vinegar	3 tbsp.	45 mL
Lemon juice	1 1/2 tsp.	7 mL
Granulated sugar	3/4 tsp.	4 mL
Pepper	3/4 tsp.	4 mL
Garlic clove, minced	1	1
Salt	3/4 tsp.	4 mL

Combine water and first amount of salt in a small saucepan. Bring to a boil. Stir in quinoa. Reduce heat to medium-low and simmer, covered, for about 20 minutes, without stirring, until quinoa is tender and liquid is absorbed. Transfer to a large bowl and set aside to cool.

Add next 7 ingredients.

Whisk remaining 7 ingredients in a small bowl. Add to quinoa mixture and toss until dressing is evenly distributed. Makes about 6 cups (1.5 L)

1 cup (250 mL): 180 Calories; 7 g Total Fat (2 g Mono, 2.5 g Poly, 1.5 g Sat); 5 mg Cholesterol; 23 g Carbohydrate (4 g Fibre, 3 g Sugar); 8 g Protein; 520 mg Sodium

Blueberry Shrimp Salad

When picking your own blueberries, either in the wild or at a berry farm, try to focus on the berries that are at their peak. Stay away from those that are green or purple, as they are not yet ripe. A perfectly ripe blueberry, whether wild or cultivated, will be blue, firm and heavy for its size. It will also burst open with flavour when you bite into it.

Grated lemon zest	1 tsp.	5 mL
Lemon juice	2 tbsp.	30 mL
Liquid honey	1 tbsp.	15 mL
Olive oil	3 tbsp.	45 mL
Salt	1/8 tsp.	0.5 mL
Pepper	1/8 tsp.	0.5 mL
Bag of fresh spring mix (8 oz., 225 g)	1	1
Cooked shrimp, peeled and deveined	1/2 lb.	225 g
Fresh blueberries	1 cup	250 mL
Feta cheese	1/2 cup	125 mL
Pecan halves	1/3 cup	75 mL

In a small bowl, combine lemon zest, lemon juice and honey, and whisk well. Add olive oil, salt and pepper, and whisk again.

Arrange salad greens on 4 plates and top with shrimp, blueberries, feta and pecans. Drizzle with dressing and serve. Makes 4 servings.

1 serving: 330 Calories; 24 g Total Fat (13 g Mono, 3.5 g Poly, 6 g Sat); 130 mg Cholesterol; 15 g Carbohydrate (4 g Fibre, 11 g Sugar); 17 g Protein; 410 mg Sodium

Beef Tenderloin with Blueberry Sauce

Beef and blueberries might seem like an odd combination, but the sweetness of the blueberries gives the tenderloin a rich, fruity flavour.

Beef tenderloin fillets (about 8 oz., 227 g, each)	4	4
Canola oil	1 tbsp.	15 mL
Salt, to taste		
Pepper, to taste		
Pieces of prosciutto (or bacon)	4	4
Butter	1 tbsp.	15 mL
Finely chopped onion	2 tbsp.	30 mL
Port wine (or red wine)	1/2 cup	125 mL
Red wine vinegar	2 tbsp.	30 mL
Red currant jelly	1 tbsp.	15 mL
Blueberries	1 cup	250 mL

Rub tenderloins with oil and season with salt and pepper. Wrap each fillet with a piece of prosciutto and secure with a toothpick. Grill beef on medium-high for 5 to 8 minutes per side, flipping once, for medium doneness. If you want to cook the meat longer, turn off grill, close lid and leave it for another 5 minutes.

For the sauce, melt butter in a small saucepan over medium and add onion. Cook until softened, about 5 minutes.

Add port wine, vinegar and jelly, and cook for 10 minutes, or until slightly reduced. Stir in berries. To serve, remove toothpicks from fillets, arrange on a plate and ladle sauce over top. Makes 4 servings.

1 serving: 540 Calories; 16 g Total Fat (5 g Mono, 1.5 g Poly, 6 g Sat); 185 mg Cholesterol; 12 g Carbohydrate (1 g Fibre, 10 g Sugar); 75 g Protein; 420 mg Sodium

Lamb Chops with Blueberry Sauce

Elegant enough for a dinner party but quick enough for a weekday meal, this delicious dish is deceptively simple to prepare.

Lamb chops (about 1 1/4 inch, 3 cm, thick), trimmed of most fat	8	8
Salt, to taste		
Pepper, to taste		
Olive oil	3 tbsp.	45 mL
Shallots, finely diced	2	2
Large celery rib, finely diced	1	1
Large parsnip, finely diced	1	1
Large carrot, finely diced	1	1
Dry red wine	2 cups	500 mL
Prepared chicken broth	4 cups	1 L
Black peppercorns	8	8
Fresh blueberries	1/2 cup	125 mL
Butter	2 tbsp.	30 mL
Fresh tarragon, finely diced	2 tbsp.	30 mL

Season lamb chops on both sides with salt and pepper. In a medium roasting pan set on 2 stove burners, heat olive oil over high. Add chops and cook for 2 to 3 minutes, until browned on one side. Turn chops over and transfer pan to oven. Cook in 400°F (200°C) oven for 5 to 6 minutes for medium-rare. Transfer 2 tbsp. (30 mL) liquid in roasting pan to a medium saucepan. Cover roasting pan and allow meat to rest.

Place saucepan with reserved liquid on a burner over high. Add shallots, celery, parsnip and carrot, and cook for about 10 minutes, until golden brown.

Add wine and cook until completely reduced. Add chicken broth and cook until reduced to 1 cup (250 mL).

Strain sauce into a small saucepan, reserving vegetables. Add peppercorns and blueberries to sauce and bring to a simmer over medium. Whisk in butter and tarragon. Serve chops drizzled with sauce and alongside vegetables. Makes 4 servings.

1 serving: 630 Calories; 33 g Total Fat (16 g Mono, 2.5 g Poly, 11 g Sat); 150 mg Cholesterol; 22 g Carbohydrate (4 g Fibre, 4 g Sugar); 43 g Protein; 1270 mg Sodium

Blueberry Meatballs

These aromatic meatballs make the perfect family meal. Kids will love the deep purple colour, and adults will appreciate the subtle ginger and lemon overtones. If you use frozen blueberries, make sure you drain them first.

Fresh (or frozen, thawed) blueberries	3/4 cup	175 mL
Soy sauce	2 tsp.	10 mL
Ground pork	1 lb.	454 g
Grated lemon zest	2 tsp.	10 mL
Minced ginger root	2 tsp.	10 mL
Pepper	1 tsp.	5 mL

Place blueberries and soy sauce in a blender or food processor and process into a sauce-like consistency.

Place ground turkey in a large bowl. Add blueberry purée, lemon zest, ginger and pepper. Mix well and form into meatballs. Place meatballs on a baking sheet. Cook in 350°F (175°C) oven for about 45 minutes, until well browned. Makes 4 servings.

1 serving: 290 Calories; 15 g Total Fat (6 g Mono, 3.5 g Poly, 4 g Sat); 115 mg Cholesterol; 5 g Carbohydrate (1 g Fibre, 3 g Sugar); 32 g Protein; 300 mg Sodium

Salmon with Blueberry Lavender Reduction

Blueberries are one of the few plants in our edible garden that are native to Canada, so they're a snap to grow. And they're so delicious eaten out of hand that we don't need to think much beyond cooking them into pancakes and pies, or perhaps adding them to a salad. But blueberries are delicious in dishes beyond salads. In this recipe we've turned them into a sauce for another Canadian native, salmon, but the sauce would be just as delicious on chicken, pork or another fish.

Fresh blueberries	1 cup	250 mL
Champagne vinegar	1 cup	250 mL
Granulated sugar	3/4 cup	175 mL
Dried lavender	1/2 tsp.	2 mL
Salt	1/4 tsp.	1 mL
Salmon fillets (6 oz., 170 g, each)	4	4
Salt, to taste		
Pepper, to taste		

Combine blueberries, champagne vinegar, sugar, lavender and first amount of salt in a small saucepan over low. Simmer until mixture is reduced by about half and coats back of a spoon. Use a wooden spoon to press sauce through a fine-mesh sieve.

While sauce is reducing, season fillets with salt and pepper. Place on a greased grill skin side up. Cook over medium-high until thinnest edge becomes opaque, 3 to 5 minutes, depending on thickness. Slip a long spatula under fillet from side, lifting entire fillet at once, to flip. If fillet sticks at all, leave it for another 30 seconds before trying again. Cook on second side only to brown outside, about 2 minutes more. To serve, place fillets on a plate and spoon sauce around fillets and over top. Makes 4 servings.

1 serving: 470 Calories; 16 g Total Fat (4.5 g Mono, 8 g Poly, 2 g Sat); 110 mg Cholesterol; 41 g Carbohydrate (trace Fibre, 40 g Sugar); 40 g Protein; 250 mg Sodium

Baked Blueberry Pecan Oatmeal

A warm, comforting breakfast casserole. Blueberries add sweetness while pecans add delectable crunch. Top with yogurt for a real treat.

Quick-cooking rolled oats	2 cups	500 mL
Milk	1 1/4 cups	300 mL
Unsweetened applesauce	3/4 cup	175 mL
Dried blueberries	1/2 cup	125 mL
Brown sugar, packed	1/4 cup	60 mL
Chopped pecans, toasted (see Tip, page 64)	1/4 cup	60 mL
Wheat germ	1/4 cup	60 mL
Butter (or hard margarine), melted	2 tbsp.	30 mL
Ground cinnamon	1 tsp.	5 mL
Vanilla extract	1 tsp.	5 mL
Ground ginger	1/2 tsp.	2 mL
Salt	1/2 tsp.	2 mL

Combine all 12 ingredients in a medium bowl. Spread evenly in a greased 8 x 8 inch (20 x 20 cm) baking dish. Bake, covered, in 350°F (175°C) oven for about 20 minutes until liquid is absorbed. Makes 4 servings.

1 serving: 460 Calories; 15 g Total Fat (5 g Mono, 2.5 g Poly, 5 g Sat); 20 mg Cholesterol; 72 g Carbohydrate (10 g Fibre, 31 g Sugar); 12 g Protein; 340 mg Sodium

Blueberry Cream Pancakes

These pancakes pack a double dose of blueberry goodness. Blueberry cream cheese gives the batter a sweet, creamy taste—and there's a good helping of fresh blueberries inside each pancake, too!

All-purpose flour	1 1/2 cups	375 mL
Granulated sugar	1 tbsp.	15 mL
Baking soda	1/4 tsp.	1 mL
Salt	1/4 tsp.	1 mL
Blueberry spreadable cream cheese	1/2 cup	125 mL
Milk	1 1/2 cups	375 mL
Large egg	1	1
Cooking oil	1 tbsp.	15 mL
Fresh (or frozen) blueberries	1 cup	250 mL

Combine first 4 ingredients in a large bowl. Make a well in centre.

Put cream cheese into a small bowl. Combine milk, egg and oil in a small bowl. Slowly add to cream cheese, whisking constantly until smooth. Add to well. Stir until just moistened. Batter will be lumpy.

Preheat griddle to medium-high. Spray with cooking spray. Pour batter onto griddle, using about 1/4 cup (60 mL) for each pancake. Scatter a few blueberries over each pancake. Cook for about 3 minutes until bubbles form on top and edges appear dry. Turn pancake over. Cook for about 3 minutes until golden. Remove to a large plate. Cover to keep warm. Repeat with remaining batter and blueberries, spraying griddle with cooking spray if necessary to prevent sticking. Makes about 12 pancakes.

1 pancake: 140 Calories; 4 g Total Fat (0.5 g Mono, 0 g Poly, 2 g Sat); 15 mg Cholesterol; 22 g Carbohydrate (1 g Fibre, 5 g Sugar); 4 g Protein; 330 mg Sodium

Blueberry Streusel French Toast

This recipe is the perfect make-ahead brunch dish. It is even better with maple or blueberry syrup drizzled on top.

Butter (or hard margarine)	1 tbsp.	15 mL
Thick bread slices (such as Texas Toast)	12	12
Large eggs	9	9
Milk	1 1/2 cups	375 mL
Granulated sugar	1 1/2 tbsp.	22 mL
Salt	1/4 tsp.	1 mL
Vanilla	1 tbsp.	15 mL
Quick-cooking rolled oats (not instant)	1 1/4 cups	300 mL
Brown sugar, packed	1/2 cup	125 mL
All-purpose flour	1/4 cup	60 mL
Finely grated lemon zest	1/2 tsp.	2 mL
Butter (or hard margarine)	1/3 cup	75 mL
Frozen (or fresh) blueberries	1 cup	250 mL

Grease an 11 x 17 inch (28 x 43 cm) baking sheet with a thick coating of butter. Arrange bread slices close to each other on baking sheet.

Beat next 5 ingredients together in a large bowl. Pour over bread slices.

For the streusel, combine rolled oats, brown sugar, flour and lemon zest in a medium bowl. Cut in butter until mixture is crumbly. Sprinkle over bread slices.

Sprinkle blueberries over streusel. Cover and chill overnight. Remove cover and bake in 450°F (230°C) oven for 30 minutes until topping is crisp and golden brown around edges. Makes 12 slices.

1 slice: 340 Calories; 13 g Total Fat (5 g Mono, 3 g Poly, 3 g Sat); 165 mg Cholesterol; 43 g Carbohydrate (4 g Fibre, 15 g Sugar); 12 g Protein; 340 mg Sodium

Blueberry Cereal Bars

Blueberries pack a nutritional wallop and are loaded with antioxidants, vitamins and fibre, an excellent reason to add them to your breakfast routine. Store in an airtight container for up to a week, or freeze for 3 to 4 months.

Whole wheat flour	1 1/2 cups	375 mL
Quick-cooking rolled oats	1 1/2 cups	375 mL
Brown sugar, firmly packed	1/2 cup	125 mL
Ground flax seed (see Tip, p. 64)	1/2 cup	125 mL
Ground cinnamon	1 tsp.	5 mL
Baking soda	1/2 tsp.	2 mL
Salt	1/4 tsp.	1 mL
Butter, cut up	1 cup	250 mL
Blueberries	2 cups	500 mL
Granulated sugar	1/3 cup	75 mL
Whole wheat flour	1 tbsp.	15 mL
Vanilla extract	1 tsp.	5 mL
Lemon juice	1 tbsp.	15 mL

In a large bowl, combine first 7 ingredients. Cut in butter until mixture resembles coarse crumbs. Press half of mixture into a 9 x 13 inch (23 x 33 cm) baking dish sprayed with cooking spray. Set remaining mixture aside.

Combine remaining 5 ingredients in a blender and process until smooth. Spread over mixture in pan. Sprinkle remaining flour mixture over top. Bake in 350°F (175°C) oven for 25 to 30 minutes until top begins to brown. Cool completely before slicing. Cuts into 12 bars.

1 bar: 350 Calories; 20 g Total Fat (5 g Mono, 3 g Poly, 11 g Sat); 45 mg Cholesterol; 39 g Carbohydrate (6 g Fibre, 18 g Sugar); 5 g Protein; 200 mg Sodium

Blueberry Oatmeal Muffins

Instead of giving in to that fatty blueberry muffin at the bakery, make your own using healthier ingredients. This remake is boosted with fibre-rich oats, low-fat yogurt and applesauce.

Large flake rolled oats	1 cup	250 mL
Low-fat vanilla yogurt	1 cup	250 mL
Grated lemon zest (see Tip, page 64)	2 tsp.	10 mL
Large eggs	2	2
Unsweetened applesauce	1/2 cup	125 mL
Canola oil	3 tbsp.	45 mL
Lemon juice	1 tbsp.	15 mL
All-purpose flour	1 1/2 cups	375 mL
Brown sugar, packed	2/3 cup	150 mL
Baking powder	2 tsp.	10 mL
Ground cinnamon	1 tsp.	5 mL
Baking soda	1/2 tsp.	2 mL
Salt	1/2 tsp.	2 mL
Fresh (or frozen) blueberries	1 1/2 cups	375 mL

Combine first 3 ingredients in a medium bowl. Let stand for 10 minutes.

Stir in next 4 ingredients.

Combine next 6 ingredients in a large bowl. Make a well in centre and add blueberries and rolled oat mixture. Stir until just moistened. Fill 12 greased muffin cups 3/4 full. Bake in 375°F (190°C) oven for about 22 minutes until wooden pick inserted in centre of muffin comes out clean. Let stand in pan for 5 minutes before removing to wire rack to cool. Makes 12 muffins.

1 muffin: 210 Calories; 5 g Total Fat (2.5 g Mono, 1.5 g Poly, 0.5 g Sat); 25 mg Cholesterol; 36 g Carbohydrate (2 g Fibre, 17 g Sugar); 4 g Protein; 220 mg Sodium

Blueberry Lemon Loaf

Light and buttery with a delicate lemon flavour, this loaf is a perfect match for vanilla ice cream.

All-purpose flour	2 cups	500 mL
Baking powder	1 1/4 tsp.	6 mL
Salt	1/2 tsp.	2 mL
Butter (or hard margarine), softened	1/2 cup	125 mL
Granulated sugar	1 cup	250 mL
Large eggs	3	3
Milk	1/2 cup	125 mL
Fresh (or frozen) blueberries	1 cup	250 mL
Grated lemon zest	1 1/2 tbsp.	22 mL
Lemon juice	1/4 cup	60 mL
Icing (confectioner's) sugar	1/4 cup	60 mL

Combine first 3 ingredients in a medium bowl. Set aside.

Cream butter and sugar in a large bowl. Add eggs 1 at a time, beating well after each addition.

Add flour mixture in 3 parts, alternating with milk in 2 parts, stirring after each addition until just combined. Add blueberries and lemon zest. Stir until just combined. Spread in a greased 9 x 5 x 3 inch (23 x 12.5 x 7.5 cm) loaf pan. Bake in 325°F (160°C) oven for 60 to 65 minutes or until wooden pick inserted in centre comes out clean.

For the glaze, stir lemon juice into icing sugar in a small bowl until smooth. Randomly poke several holes in loaf with a wooden pick. Spoon glaze over hot loaf. Let stand in pan until cooled completely. Cuts into 16 slices.

1 slice: 200 Calories; 8 g Total Fat (2 g Mono, 0 g Poly, 4.5 g Sat); 55 mg Cholesterol; 30 g Carbohydrate (1 g Fibre, 16 g Sugar); 4 g Protein; 105 mg Sodium

Blueberry Fruit Leather

You might call fruit leather "vegetarian beef jerky." It is an intriguing treat that, although especially popular with children, is appreciated by people of all ages. You can make this recipe in advance and, after the fruit leather has been cut into strips, wrap each one individually. Pack them along on a picnic lunch as a snack. Feel free to switch out some of the blueberries for another of your favourite berries; raspberries would be a great addition.

Crushed fresh blueberries	4 cup	1 L
Granulated sugar	1/2 cup	125 mL
Applesauce	2 cups	500 mL

Stir crushed berries and sugar together in a medium saucepan over medium until sugar has dissolved. Put mixture through a food mill or sieve to remove any stems.

Add applesauce and mix well. Pour onto a greased rimmed baking sheet and spread mixture to an even thickness. Place in a food dehydrator, or in 175°F (80°C) oven, for 5 to 6 hours, until firm to the touch and dry enough to peel off baking sheet. Let cool completely. Use scissors to cut fruit leather into strips, and store strips in an airtight container or bag. Cuts into 20 pieces.

2 pieces: 100 Calories; 0 g Total Fat (0 g Mono, 0 g Poly, 0 g Sat); 0 mg Cholesterol; 25 g Carbohydrate (2 g Fibre, 22 g Sugar); 1 g Protein; 0 mg Sodium

Blueberry Shortcakes

Delightful little scone-like cakes topped with fresh berries and whipped cream. The perfect summer treat.

Fresh blueberries	6 cups	1.5 L
Granulated sugar	1/4 cup	60 mL
Lemon juice	1 tbsp.	15 mL
Whipping cream	1 1/4 cups	300 mL
Granulated sugar	2 tbsp.	30 mL
All-purpose baking flour	2 1/4 cups	550 mL
Granulated sugar	1/4 cup	60 mL
Baking powder	2 tsp.	10 mL
Baking soda	1/2 tsp.	2 mL
Salt	1/2 tsp.	2 mL
Cold butter, cut up	1/2 cup	125 mL
Large egg	1	1
Whipping cream	3/4 cup	175 mL
Lemon juice	1 tbsp.	15 mL
Grated lemon zest (see Tip, p. 64)	1 tsp.	5 mL
Granulated sugar	1 tsp.	5 mL

Crush 1 1/2 cups (375 mL) blueberries in a medium bowl. Stir in first amounts of sugar and lemon juice and remaining blueberries. Set aside.

Beat first amount of whipping cream and second amount of sugar in a small bowl until stiff peaks form. Chill.

Combine next 5 ingredients in a medium bowl. Cut in butter until mixture resembles coarse crumbs. Make a well in centre.

Combine next 4 ingredients in a small bowl. Add to well and stir until just moistened. Turn out dough onto a lightly floured surface. Knead 8 to 10 times. Roll or pat out to 1 inch (2.5 cm) thickness. Cut into eight 3 inch (7.5 cm) circles using a lightly floured biscuit cutter. Arrange about 1 1/2 inches (3.8 cm) apart on a greased baking sheet.

Sprinkle with fourth amount of sugar. Bake in 400°F (200°C) oven for about 14 minutes until wooden pick inserted in centre of biscuit comes out clean.

Transfer to a wire rack to cool slightly. Split biscuits in half horizontally. Transfer to plates. Spoon blueberry mixture onto biscuit bottoms. Top with whipped cream mixture. Set biscuit tops over whipped cream. Makes 8 shortcakes.

1 shortcake: 550 Calories; 32 g Total Fat (9 g Mono, 1.5 g Poly, 20 g Sat); 100 mg Cholesterol; 64 g Carbohydrate (5 g Fibre, 26 g Sugar); 6 g Protein; 390 mg Sodium

Blueberry Clafouti

A quick frying pan method leads to a delightful dessert in just a of couple minutes.

Butter (or hard margarine)	1 tbsp.	15 mL
Frozen blueberries pieces	1 1/2 cups	375 mL
Large eggs	2	2
Milk	1 cup	250 mL
All-purpose flour	1/2 cup	125 mL
Granulated sugar	1/4 cup	60 mL
Baking powder	1 tsp.	5 mL
Ground cinnamon	1/8 tsp.	0.5 mL
Salt	1/8 tsp.	0.5 mL
Granulated sugar	1 tsp.	5 mL

Melt butter in a medium frying pan on medium. Add blueberries and cook for about 3 minutes, stirring occasionally, until heated through.

Beat next 7 ingredients in a medium bowl until smooth. Slowly pour over blueberry mixture. Do not stir. Cook, covered, for about 5 minutes until almost set. Remove from heat. Broil, uncovered, on centre rack in oven for about 7 minutes until knife inserted in centre of custard comes out clean (see Tip, 64).

Sprinkle with second amount of sugar. Cuts into 4 wedges.

1 wedge: 230 Calories; 6 g Total Fat (1.5 g Mono, 0.5 g Poly, 3 g Sat); 80 mg Cholesterol; 38 g Carbohydrate (2 g Fibre, 23 g Sugar); 7 g Protein; 220 mg Sodium

Blueberry Pecan Cake

This moist, tender cake is just bursting with blueberries. It is delicious on its own or topped with whipped cream.

All-purpose flour	1 cup	250 mL
Butter (or hard margarine), softened	1/2 cup	125 mL
Brown sugar, packed	1/3 cup	75 mL
Medium coconut	1/4 cup	60 mL
Lemon zest	1 tsp.	5 mL
Granulated sugar	3/4 cup	175 mL
Butter (or hard margarine), softened	1/4 cup	60 mL
Large egg	1	1
Sour cream	1/2 cup	125 mL
All-purpose flour	1 1/2 cups	375 mL
Baking powder	2 tsp.	10 mL
Salt	1 tsp.	5 mL
Frozen blueberries, thawed and drained (or fresh)	2 cups	500 mL
Coarsely chopped pecans	1/2 cup	125 mL
Whipped cream (optional)	2 cups	500 mL

For the crumb topping, combine first 5 ingredients in a small bowl. Mix until crumbly. Set aside.

For the cake, cream sugar and butter in a large bowl until smooth. Beat in egg and sour cream.

Combine next 3 ingredients in a small bowl. Gradually stir into butter mixture, stirring until just combined.

Fold in blueberries and pecans. Turn into a greased 8 x 8 inch (20 x 20 cm) pan. Sprinkle with topping. Bake in 350°F (175°C) oven for 50 to 60 minutes until wooden pick inserted in center comes out clean.

Serve with whipped cream, if using. Cuts into 9 pieces.

1 piece: 510 Calories; 27 g Total Fat (12 g Mono, 5 g Poly, 7 g Sat); 30 mg Cholesterol; 61 g Carbohydrate (3 g Fibre, 27 g Sugar); 6 g Protein; 600 mg Sodium

Blueberry Lemon Layer Cake

This lovely cake is sweet yet tangy. The lemon cream cheese icing elevates this cake from delicious to outstanding. You'll need about 3 medium lemons for this recipe.

Butter (or hard margarine), softened	1 cup	250 mL
Granulated sugar	1 cup	250 mL
Brown sugar, packed	1/2 cup	125 mL
Large eggs	4	4
Vanilla extract	2 tsp.	10 mL
All-purpose flour	3 cups	750 mL
Baking powder	1 tbsp.	15 mL
Salt	1/2 tsp.	2 mL
Buttermilk	1 cup	250 mL
Lemon juice	1/2 cup	125 mL
Grated lemon zest	1 tbsp.	15 mL
Fresh (or frozen) blueberries	1 1/2 cups	375 mL
All-purpose flour	1 tbsp.	15 mL
Cream cheese, softened	12 oz.	340 g
Butter (or hard margarine), softened	1/2 cup	125 mL
Icing (confectioner's) sugar	4 1/2 cups	1.1 L
Grated lemon zest	1 tsp.	5 mL
Lemon juice	1 tbsp.	15 mL
Milk	2 tbsp.	30 mL
Vanilla extract	1 tsp.	5 mL

Cream first amount of butter and both sugars in a large bowl. Add eggs, 1 at a time, beating well after each addition. Add vanilla. Beat until smooth.

Combine next 3 ingredients in a medium bowl. Gradually stir into butter mixture, stirring until just combined. Stir in next 3 ingredients, stirring until just combined.

Combine blueberries and remaining flour in a small bowl. Fold into batter. Do not overmix. Divide evenly into to 3 greased 9 inch (23 cm) round pans. Bake in 350°F (175°C) oven for about 20 minutes, until wooden pick inserted in centre comes out clean. Set aside to cool.

For the icing, beat cream cheese and remaining butter in a large bowl until light and fluffy. Add next 3 ingredients and beat on low until combined. Increase speed to medium and beat until creamy. Add milk and vanilla and beat until light and fluffy. Place 1 cake on a serving plate. If cake is too round on top, use a serrated knife to trim top. Spread with icing. Repeat with remaining cakes and icing. Spread icing on top and sides of cake. Cuts into 16 wedges.

1 wedge: 496 Calories; 20 g Total Fat (5 g Mono, 1 g Poly, 12 g Sat); 103 mg Cholesterol; 72 g Carbohydrate (1 g Fibre, 50 g Sugar); 8 g Protein; 417 mg Sodium

Fresh Blueberry Pie

This pie is excellent served warm with a scoop of ice cream or cold with whipped cream.

Pastry for 2 crust 9 inch (23 cm) pie	1	1
Granulated sugar	1 cup	250 mL
All-purpose flour	1/4 cup	60 mL
Ground cinnamon	1/4 tsp.	1 mL
Salt	1/4 tsp.	1 mL
Fresh blueberries	4 cups	1 L
Lemon juice	1 1/2 tbsp.	22 mL
Granulated sugar	1/2 tsp.	2 mL

Divide pastry into 2 portions, making 1 portion slightly larger than the other. Shape each portion into a slightly flattened disc. Roll out larger portion on a lightly floured surface to about 1/8 inch (3 mm) thickness. Line a 9 inch (23 cm) pie plate.

Combine next 4 ingredients in a large bowl. Stir in blueberries. Spread evenly in shell.

Drizzle lemon juice over top. Roll out smaller pastry portion on a lightly floured surface to about 1/8 inch (3 mm) thickness. Dampen edge of pastry shell with water. Cover with pastry. Trim and crimp decorative edge to seal. Cut several small vents in top to allow steam to escape.

Sprinkle with sugar. Bake on bottom rack in 350°F (175°C) oven for about 50 minutes until browned and fruit is tender. Cuts into 8 wedges.

1 wedge: 490 Calories; 19 g Total Fat (0 g Mono, 0 g Poly, 4.5 g Sat); 25 mg Cholesterol; 79 g Carbohydrate (4 g Fibre, 36 g Sugar); 3 g Protein; 410 mg Sodium

Creamy Berry Crisps

No one would ever believe that you made these delicious fruit crisps in just a couple minutes.

Quick-cooking rolled oats	1 cup	250 mL
Brown sugar, packed	1/4 cup	60 mL
Butter (or hard margarine)	3 tbsp.	45 mL
Ground cinnamon	1/2 tsp.	2 mL
Block cream cheese, softened	4 oz.	125 g
Granulated sugar	1/2 cup	125 mL
Frozen blueberries	1 1/2 cups	375 mL
Frozen raspberries	1/2 cup	125 mL

Toast rolled oats in a large frying pan on medium, stirring constantly, for about 5 minutes until starting to turn golden. Add next 3 ingredients. Heat, stirring, for 1 to 2 minutes until mixture is browned and crisp. Remove from heat.

Combine cream cheese and granulated sugar in a medium bowl.

Add berries and stir until coated. Spoon into 4 greased 3/4 cup (175 mL) ramekins. Microwave, covered, on high (100%) for about 3 minutes until bubbling and heated through (see Tip, p. 64). Spoon oat mixture over top. Makes 4 crisps.

1 crisp: 430 Calories; 20 g Total Fat (3 g Mono, 1 g Poly, 12 g Sat); 55 mg Cholesterol; 61 g Carbohydrate (4 g Fibre, 45 g Sugar); 5 g Protein; 160 mg Sodium

Blueberry Ice Cream

Rich and decadent, this ice cream beats anything you could find in your local supermarket.

Whole milk	1 cup	250 mL
Heavy cream	3 cups	750 mL
Vanilla bean, split lengthwise	1	1
Egg yolks	5	5
Granulated sugar	3/4 cup	175 mL
Blueberries	2 1/2 cups	625 mL

In a heavy-bottomed saucepan, heat milk, cream and vanilla bean until just before boiling, stirring occasionally. Remove from heat and remove vanilla bean. Scrape out seeds and add them to milk. Set aside.

In a mixing bowl, whisk egg yolks and sugar until pale yellow and thickened. Slowly pour about 1 cup (250 mL) of hot cream mixture into egg yolks, whisking constantly. Add yolk mixture back into remaining cream and cook over medium heat, stirring constantly, until mixture thickens and coats back of spoon. Do not let mixture boil at any time or it will curdle. Pour through a fine-mesh sieve into a bowl.

Add blueberries and freeze in ice cream maker according to manufacturer's instructions. Makes 4 cups.

1/2 cup (125 ml): 310 Calories; 19 g Total Fat (6 g Mono, 1 g Poly, 11 g Sat); 180 mg Cholesterol; 31 g Carbohydrate (1 g Fibre, 25 g Sugar); 6 g Protein; 55 mg Sodium

Blueberry Cream Frappé

With flavours reminiscent of blueberry tea, this creamy drink is totally chilled out. To make a more grown-up version, try using 1 or 2 tbsp. (15 to 30 mL) of amaretto in place of the almond extract.

Frozen blueberries	3 cups	750 mL
Milk	1 cup	250 mL
Crushed ice (or 4 ice cubes)	1/2 cup	125 mL
Orange juice	1/2 cup	125 mL
Vanilla yogurt	1/2 cup	125 mL
Almond extract	1/2 tsp.	2 mL

Process all 6 ingredients in a blender until smooth. Makes about 4 cups (1 L).

2/3 cup (150 ml): 80 Calories; 1 g Total Fat (0 g Mono, 0 g Poly, 0.5 g Sat); 1 mg Cholesterol; 14 g Carbohydrate (2 g Fibre, 11 g Sugar); 3 g Protein; 40 mg Sodium

Pomegranate Berry Smoothie

This fruit smoothie is a great choice for anyone who is interested in adding greens to smoothies but is hesitant to try. The rich flavours of acai, pomegranate and blueberries can mask almost any green you want to add—frozen peas also work well. Or you can leave the veggies out and enjoy a tasty fruity treat.

Fresh (or frozen) blueberries	2 cups	500 mL
Baby spinach, optional	1 cup	250 mL
Acai powder	1 tbsp.	15 mL
Hemp protein powder	1 tbsp.	15 mL
Pomegranate berry juice	1 cup	250 mL
Ice cubes	1 cup	250 mL

Combine berries, spinach (if using), acai, hemp and pomegranate juice in a blender until smooth. Add ice and blend again until smooth and icy. Makes 2 servings.

1 serving: 180 Calories; 1 g Total Fat (0 g Mono, 0 g Poly, 0 g Sat); 0 mg Cholesterol; 44 g Carbohydrate (5 g Fibre, 36 g Sugar); 3 g Protein; 20 mg Sodium

Blueberry Chocolate Bean Smoothie

Blending beans into a smoothie might seem a little odd, but the end result is rich, creamy and loaded with nutrition. White beans such as navy or cannellini beans are excellent sources of fibre and folate, both of which are often lacking in the typical North American diet, and are high in protein, iron, potassium and manganese. This is another smoothie that lends itself to hiding greens; baby spinach works especially well.

Frozen blueberries	1 cup	250 mL
Cacao nibs	1/4 cup	60 mL
Canned white beans	1/4 cup	60 mL
Vanilla Greek yogurt	1/2 cup	125 mL
Almond milk	1 cup	250 mL

Combine all 5 ingredients in a blender until smooth. Makes 2 servings.

1 serving: 290 Calories; 11 g Total Fat (1 g Mono, 0 g Poly, 6 g Sat); 5 mg Cholesterol; 28 g Carbohydrate (9 g Fibre, 15 g Sugar); 14 g Protein; 170 mg Sodium

Blueberry Salsa

This salsa makes a great side dish, or use it as a topping for savoury grilled dishes. It goes particularly well with fish.

Lime juice	1 tbsp.	15 mL
Salt	1/2 tsp.	2 mL
Cilantro	1/4 cup	60 mL
Minced hot chili pepper	2 tsp.	10 mL
Blueberries	2 cups	500 mL
Diced jicama, cut into 1/4 in (5 mm) pieces	1/2 cup	125 mL
Green onions, thinly sliced	2	2

Combine lime juice and salt in a medium bowl. Stir until salt has dissolved.

Stir in cilantro and chili pepper. Add blueberries, jicama and green onion and toss to combine. Makes 3 cups (750 mL).

1/2 cup (125 ml): 50 Calories; 0.5 g Total Fat (0 g Mono, 0 g Poly, 0 g Sat); 0 mg Cholesterol; 11 g Carbohydrate (4 g Fibre, 6 g Sugar); 2 g Protein; 190 mg Sodium

Peach Blueberry Jam

Summer's favourite flavours combine in this colourful jam. This sweet spread is made even better with the additions of lime and vanilla.

Finely chopped peeled peach (see Tip, page 64)	3 cups	750 mL
Crushed fresh (or frozen, thawed) blueberries	1 1/4 cups	300 mL
Lime juice	3 tbsp.	45 mL
Box of pectin crystals (2 oz., 57 g)	1	1
Grated lime zest (see Tip, page 64)	1 tsp.	5 mL
Vanilla bean, split	1/2	1/2
Granulated sugar	5 cups	1.25 L

Stir first 6 ingredients in Dutch oven until pectin is dissolved. Bring to a boil, stirring constantly.

Add sugar. Bring to a hard boil, stirring constantly. Boil hard for 1 minute, stirring constantly. Remove from heat. Remove and discard vanilla bean. Skim and discard foam. Fill 6 hot sterile 1 cup (250 mL) jars to within 1/4 inch (6 mm) of top. Remove air bubbles and adjust headspace if necessary. Wipe rims. Place hot metal lids on jars and screw on metal bands fingertip tight. Do not over-tighten. Process in a boiling water bath for 15 minutes. Remove jars and let stand at room temperature until cool. Makes about 6 cups (1.5 L).

1 tbsp. (15 mL): 45 Calories; 0 g Total Fat (0 g Mono, 0 g Poly, 0 g Sat); 0 mg Cholesterol; 12 g Carbohydrate (0 g Fibre, 11 g Sugar); 0 g Protein; 0 mg Sodium

Blueberry Orange Freezer Jam

This freezer jam is equally delicious with fresh or frozen blueberries.
If you've got berries on hand in the summer, try the fresh version. With
frozen berries, you'll get a deep blueberry flavour. Double the recipe if
you want to use the entire package of pectin.

Granulated sugar	3/4 cup	175 mL
Envelope of freezer jam pectin	1/2	1/2
(1.59 oz., 45 g)		
Crushed blueberries	1 1/2 cups	375 mL
Finely chopped orange segments	1/2 cup	125 mL
(see Tip, 64)		
Orange liqueur	1 tbsp.	15 mL
Grated orange zest (see Tip, page 64)	1 tsp.	5 mL

Combine sugar and pectin in a medium bowl.

Add remaining 4 ingredients. Stir for 3 minutes. Fill clean plastic containers to within 1/2 inch (12 mm) of top. Wipe rims. Let stand at room temperature for about 30 minutes until thickened. Cover with tight-fitting lids. Store in refrigerator for up to 3 weeks or in freezer for up to 1 year. Makes about 2 1/4 cups (550 mL).

1 tbsp. (15 mL): 20 Calories; 0 g Total Fat (0 g Mono, 0 g Poly, 0 g Sat); 0 mg Cholesterol; 5 g Carbohydrate (0 g Fibre, 5 g Sugar); 0 g Protein; 0 mg Sodium

Bumbleberry Sauce

Capture the flavours of summer in this sweet-tart blend of berries in a luscious sauce. Perfect for serving over ice cream, angel food cake, yogurt or granola. Use any mix of berries as long as the total volume adds up to 4 1/2 cups (1.1 L).

Fresh blueberries	1 1/2 cups	375 mL
Fresh (or frozen) raspberries	1 1/2 cups	375 mL
Halved fresh strawberries	1 1/2 cups	375 mL
Mixed berry juice (no sugar added)	1 cup	250 mL
Grated lemon zest	1 tsp.	5 mL
Granulated sugar	3/4 cup	175 mL
Corn syrup	1/3 cup	75 mL
Bottled lemon juice	3 tbsp.	45 mL

Combine first 5 ingredients in a large saucepan. Bring to a boil on medium, crushing occasionally with potato masher to break up berries.

Add sugar, stirring constantly until dissolved.

Add corn syrup and lemon juice. Bring to a hard boil, stirring constantly. Boil hard for 5 minutes, stirring often. Fill 4 hot sterile 1 cup (250 mL) jars to within 1/4 inch (6 mm) of top. Remove air bubbles and adjust headspace if necessary. Wipe rims. Place hot metal lids on jars and screw on metal bands fingertip tight. Do not over-tighten. Process in a boiling water bath for 15 minutes. Remove jars and let stand at room temperature until cool. Makes about 4 1/2 cups (1.1 L).

2 tbsp. (30 mL): 35 Calories; 0 g Total Fat (0 g Mono, 0 g Poly, 0 g Sat); 0 mg Cholesterol; 9 g Carbohydrate (1 g Fibre, 8 g Sugar); 0 g Protein; 0 mg Sodium

recipe index

topical tips

Broiling: When baking or broiling food in a frying pan with a handle that isn't ovenproof, wrap the handle in foil and keep it to the front of the oven, away from the element.

Grinding flaxseed: To make 1/4 cup (60 mL) ground flaxseed, grind 2 1/2 tbsp. (37 mL) whole flaxseed in a blender or coffee grinder. Store in airtight container in the refrigerator.

Microwave powers: The microwaves used in our test kitchen are 900 watts—but microwaves are sold in many different powers. You should be able to find the wattage of yours by opening the door and looking for the mandatory label. If your microwave is more or less than 900 watts, you may need adjust the cooking time accordingly.

Peeling fresh fruit: To peel fresh fruit and produce more easily, blanch in boiling water for 30 to 60 seconds. Immediately plunge into cold water and remove skins.

Segmenting fruit: To segment citrus fruits, trim a small slice of peel from both ends so the flesh is exposed. Place the fruit, bottom cut-side down, on a cutting board. Remove the peel with a sharp knife, cutting down and around the flesh, leaving as little pith as possible. Over a small bowl, cut on either side of the membranes to release the segments.

Toasting pecans: To toast pecans, place them in an ungreased frying pan. Heat on medium, stirring often, until golden.

Toasting pine nuts: Pine nuts have a relatively high oil content and burn easily, so take care when toasting them.

Zesting fruit: When a recipe calls for both grated zest and juice, it's easier to grate the fruit first, then juice it. Be careful not to grate down to the pith, which is bitter and is best avoided.

Nutrition Information Guidelines

Each recipe is analyzed using the Canadian Nutrient File from Health Canada, which is based on the United States Department of Agriculture (USDA) Nutrient Database.

- If more than one ingredient is listed (such as "butter or hard margarine"), or if a range is given (1 – 2 tsp., 5 – 10 mL), only the first ingredient or first amount is analyzed.

- For meat, poultry and fish, the serving size per person is based on the recommended 4 oz. (113 g) uncooked weight (without bone), which is 2 – 3 oz. (57 – 85 g) cooked weight (without bone) — approximately the size of a deck of playing cards.

- Milk used is 1% M.F. (milk fat), unless otherwise stated.

- Cooking oil used is canola oil, unless otherwise stated.

- Ingredients indicating "sprinkle," "optional" or "for garnish" are not included in the nutrition information.

- The fat in recipes and combination foods can vary greatly depending on the sources and types of fats used in each specific ingredient. For these reasons, the count of saturated, monounsaturated and polyunsaturated fats may not add up to the total fat content.